John and Jane

To great friends and fellow Los Alamos residents. You are here living the Wonder Years with me.

THE WONDER YEARS

PORTRAITS OF ATHLETES WHO NEVER SLOW DOWN

THE WONDER YEARS

PORTRAITS OF ATHLETES WHO NEVER SLOW DOWN

by **RICK RICKMAN** and **DONNA WARES**

Foreword by **PEGGY FLEMING**

CHRONICLE BOOKS
SAN FRANCISCO

Library of Congress Cataloging-in-Publication Data available.

ISBN: 978-0-8118-6849-5

Manufactured in China.

Designed by Empire Design Studio

10 9 8 7 6 5 4 3 2 1

Chronicle Books LLC
680 Second Street
San Francisco, California 94107

www.chroniclebooks.com

*To the athletes and adventurers who
inspired and humbled us daily*

CONTENTS

FOREWORD

Peggy Fleming

WE'RE ALL KEY PLAYERS IN THE GAME OF LIFE. AS ATHLETES, WE LOVE A CHALLENGE—FROM OUR FIRST TASTE OF COMPETITION, DEFEAT, AND VICTORY, OUR EXPERIENCES AS CHILDREN SHAPE WHO WE ARE AND WHAT DRIVES US TO SET GOALS AND ACHIEVE SUCCESS. BEING INVOLVED IN SPORTS TESTS EVERYTHING ABOUT US—PHYSICALLY, MENTALLY, AND EMOTIONALLY—BUT WE KEEP GOING BECAUSE WE KNOW THE THRILL OF POWERING THROUGH UNTIL THE VERY END. WE HAVE THE DRIVE, THE AMBITION, AND THE WILL TO STEP UP TO THE PLATE AND GIVE OUR ALL.

But now what?

When we get older, does that mean we have to give up on that euphoric feeling of empowerment we find through sports and exercise? Are we expected to lose passion for what we've always loved? The answer is most obviously: *No way. Not on your life*! We'll never stop because it's a part of our identity, our mind, and our spirit.

When I won an Olympic Gold medal for figure skating in 1968, it helped define who I was to the world and to my friends, family, and coaches. It didn't, however, ensure that life would be a cakewalk. It put pressure on me to achieve and win. But that's not why I continued for the next forty years to train, to exercise, or to run seven miles when I really wanted to take the morning off and get a pedicure. I did it because I knew it made me stronger, healthier, happier. That joy and satisfaction carried over into everything else in my

life. An Olympic medal is only a physical representation of the internal drive that athletes everywhere, at every age, carry with them in the pool, on the court, or on the rink. Strong will pushes us to get back into those running clothes, even if they've gotten a little tight, or to commit to weight training, even if we can't lift what we used to. It's the constant reinvention of who we are now—not who we were back then— that keeps us going.

Today, thanks to medicine and technology, good eating habits, and active lifestyles, we're living longer and we're happier into the later years than our parents' generation. While our culture worships the physical images of youth, we're a part of an older population that knows what youth still feels like, even if we've pushed the half-century mark! Many of us are in on the secret to happiness, which is not a number but a feeling. And

believe me, as we get older, we pay attention to numbers: cholesterol, heart, blood, stress levels, cell counts . . . you name it, it's important to know it all. But those numbers don't represent how you feel on the inside. They don't quantify the dreams you still hold on to, or the goals you've set for yourself.

This book's moving collection of photographs and stories captures the joy and exhilaration of life, the energy of competition, and the pride of accomplishment. Rick's photographs showcase a fresh look at the wrinkled face of determination, revealing that beauty is timeless and athleticism truly never fades. His work proves that, at any stage of the game, life can be filled with excitement, action, and an ageless love for adrenaline. *The Wonder Years* will change how you look at seniors and alter your perception of what the future may hold for you.

This is the time to keep testing ourselves, to take new risks mentally and physically. Staying involved and active is what life is all about and is what makes me feel alive and young. We are the only ones who know how we feel, how strong we are, and what we are made of. The fountain of youth is not a pill or a cream—it's you. You hold the key to getting what you want out of life. Don't just sit back and wonder what it could be like, just jump in and participate. You might surprise yourself.

I invite you to be inspired by those around you and by the amazing athletes featured in this book. This is their story as well as yours!

INTRODUCTION

Rick Rickman

AMERICA HAS ALWAYS WORSHIPPED YOUTH. THIS ATTITUDE PERMEATES OUR FILMS AND SPORTS AND CULTURE, AS IF OUR FONDEST WISH IS NEVER TO GROW UP—WHICH IS, OF COURSE, A FUTILE DESIRE, DESTINED FOR DISAPPOINTMENT. BUT AS AMERICA GRAYS, SOME MEN AND WOMEN ARE DISCOVERING A BETTER ALTERNATIVE: GROWING OLDER, BUT CONTINUING TO GROW. TO LIVE LIFE TO ITS FULLEST. TO *PLAY*.

They have discovered something better than a fountain of youth: They have made their later years their wonder years.

They may seem like ordinary people, with bills and mortgages and extended families spread across the map, but they also have nurtured within themselves a relentless determination to tackle new challenges every day. Some find their challenge in the gym or on the track. Others surf, swim, vault, or even rope cattle.

Raising the bar ever higher is what keeps them going and constantly growing, breaking barriers, setting records, exceeding expectations—and showing the rest of us the way.

They show us that aging isn't something to fear—it's a chance to reinvent yourself, as many times as you dare. These adventurers in their seventh, eighth, and ninth decades of life are stars in a growing senior underground that has flourished while hardly anyone paid attention. And once you meet these folks, once you take in their accomplishments, their grace, and their joy at striving for their best each day, you can't help but be inspired to find your own wonder years.

For the past two decades, I've traveled the country chronicling the lives of aging adventurers and amateur athletes who defy the conventional wisdom about what it means to grow old in our society. Their stories dramatically illustrate what medical studies and common sense tell us: People who exercise regularly live longer, live better, and, more often than not, enjoy better relationships in their later years.

Growing up, I always found it odd that people feared aging. I owe that to my grandfather, Jake. He farmed corn and soybeans in Iowa, and worked hard all his life, but when he retired, he never sat still. Jake taught himself how to become an auto mechanic—not because he had to, but because he wanted to. He helped fix most of his neighbors' cars and did it for the sheer joy of learning new things. Instead of hiring a contractor to build his new house, he taught himself how to take on the job, then rounded up family members and friends to help put up a three-bedroom home on Spirit Lake. My grandfather had more stamina and more exuberance for life than men twenty or thirty years his junior. Watching him, I began to understand

that there are no real impediments at any age to learning, growth, or fun. For Jake, growing older simply meant he could finally do the things he had always wanted to do.

Years later, when I worked as a newspaper photographer in Iowa and then in California, I developed an interest in the exploits of older athletes, and this evolved into my becoming the official photographer for the National Senior Games. I have learned that vigorous seniors like my grandfather, who lived until a healthy age of ninety-four, actually aren't that unusual. What is unusual is to read about them or see them featured in any meaningful way in our youth-obsessed media and culture. During the summer of 2008, network broadcasters kept marveling and shaking their heads in disbelief when a forty-one-year-old American woman qualified for the U.S. Olympic swimming team heading to Beijing. Since when did we collectively decide that our expectation for greatness fades by forty? Or fifty? Or even eighty? The reality is that our entire population—seniors included—now benefits from unprecedented advances in nutrition, health, and medical research, and endless opportunities for staying fit. Who knows how far America's seventy-six million people over age fifty could go if more of them got up off the couch and put aside the remote control?

I first heard about the National Senior Games in May of 1989, when I read a story buried in the sports section that mentioned a new event for athletes over age fifty. The article was small, but the games were not: more than three thousand athletes from across the country had qualified in track and field, swimming, softball, basketball, archery, volleyball, and other events. They were gathering in St. Louis for the National Senior Games, the country's second-ever Senior Olympics. I had to know more.

When I arrived in St. Louis that summer, an air of excitement filled the stadium—of serious competition by athletes having the times of their lives before cheering sections packed with spouses, grown children, and grandchildren, too. For some, the games offered a chance to recapture old glory. For others, it was a first exhilarating experience, and one that had been a long time coming: a number of the women athletes had grown up in an era when girls were denied opportunities to compete on the diamond, the track, and the court.

Since those games, I've returned again and again to the National Senior Games, savoring my role as official photographer. Each year the number of athletes multiplies, the events list expands, and the competition grows more intense as the national games make their way around the country, bound for the San Francisco Bay Area in 2009, Houston in 2011, and Cleveland in 2013. More than three hundred thousand seniors now vie at the local and state levels for a chance to compete in the nationals.

In the photographs and stories that follow, you'll find some memorable moments from the Senior Olympics, along with portraits of other extraordinary seniors I have met in my travels. All of these seniors share some common traits, among them the determination to keep chasing their goals year after year and the ability to tune out well-meaning loved ones and an often patronizing culture that tell them it's time to slow down.

Slowing down simply isn't an option for people like Sister Madonna Buder, a Catholic nun who keeps blazing trails for women athletes over age seventy. Or Granville Coggs, a practicing radiologist and Congressional Gold Medal winner who didn't take up competitive running until his seventies. Or surfer Eve Fletcher, who is in her eighties and still riding the waves every week at the same Southern California beach she has surfed for the past fifty years, breaking down barriers first as a young woman surfer and now as a senior citizen.

Every fifty seconds someone in the United States turns fifty. The upper end of the boomer generation has hit retirement age and can expect to live longer than any previous generation. The average human life expectancy now hovers around seventy-eight. Popular culture sometimes suggests there is little to look forward to in those later years, but popular culture is wrong. The men and women featured in this book have a different message, one of grace and style, a path to the wonder years.

THEY HAVE MADE THEIR LATER YEARS THEIR WONDER YEARS.

JANET FREEMAN

JANET FREEMAN NEVER HAD A CHANCE TO PLAY ORGANIZED SPORTS
GROWING UP IN SOUTH HAVEN, MICHIGAN, A SMALL TOWN WITH NO TEAMS
FOR GIRLS OR ENCOURAGEMENT FOR THOSE WITH A DESIRE TO COMPETE.
SO SHE JOINED THE CHEERLEADING SQUAD AND SCHOOL BAND INSTEAD,
AND STOOD ON THE SIDELINES WATCHING THE BOYS. SHE RECALLS
GLANCING LONGINGLY AT THE PARALLEL BARS AND POMMEL HORSE IN
THE SCHOOL GYM, BUT THOSE, TOO, WERE OFF-LIMITS TO HER.

After high school, Freeman went right to work as a waitress. She married a young schoolteacher and moved to Napoleon, Ohio, where they raised two sons and two daughters. By then she was too busy to think about sports, aside from the occasional bowling night.

Then one weekend, when she was forty-eight, Freeman volunteered to hand out water at a 10K race sponsored by the local Lions Club. Something unexpectedly clicked that morning as the throngs of sweaty, exuberant runners streamed past her.

After the race, she announced, "I'm going to try to be on the other side of the table next time."

The following fall, in 1981, Freeman ran in the Lions 10K and just kept going. She surprised and impressed her husband when she started jogging six to eight miles

At age fifty-seven, Freeman competed for the first time in the National Senior Games in St. Louis and has returned seven times since then. One of her biggest thrills came in 1991, when she won the Outstanding Athlete Award at the Senior Olympics in Syracuse, New York. That year, she competed in fourteen events—running 100-meter, 200-meter, 400-meter, 800-meter, and 1500-meter races, along with six swimming events, two bicycle races, and a triathlon. She returned home with four gold medals, four silver medals, and three bronze medals. She went on to compete in Baton Rouge, San Antonio, Tucson, Orlando, Hampton Roads (Virginia), and Pittsburgh.

"It just kind of snowballed," Freeman says in her quiet, understated way. "All of a sudden I went to the regionals. I won

fan is husband Don, who gave her diamond earrings for luck years ago, and she delights in wearing them when she competes. Don Freeman, who is nearly blind, volunteers as his wife's pack mule at every competition. She drives and he lugs the gear.

The couple divides their time between Ohio and Ft. Myers Beach, Florida, where they stay in an RV park from November through April. Freeman looks forward to the balmy winters along the Gulf Coast, where she trains in the sunshine every day far from the freezing Midwest temperatures.

In the summer of 2007, she underwent colon surgery. Unexpected complications forced Freeman to stop running for a while, and she feared her competitive days were over.

She began training again slowly, using a treadmill at home. When Freeman arrived in Florida in November, the warm climate proved to be her best therapy once again. She set out for leisurely bike rides along the road to Sanibel Island and started playing some "gentle" tennis with a few friends. By the end of April, she was up to playing three "hard sets of tennis," and her doctor cleared her to get behind the wheel for the drive back home to Napoleon. But he suggested that she make the trip in three days instead of her usual two.

Freeman has continued playing competitive tennis and loves it. She is weighing the possibility of trying a new sport for the National Senior Games.

"You never know what might happen," she says.

"I DIDN'T HAVE ANY EXPECTATIONS. I BROKE SOME RECORDS AND **HAD A GOOD TIME.**"

in the morning and later began bicycling all over and practicing her butterfly and freestyle strokes in Bauman Lake. Over the next few years, she found new energy and confidence as a slimmed-down competitor who cleaned up in races across town and across the state.

everything. So I went to state. Then I went to nationals. I didn't have any expectations. I broke some records and had a good time."

Freeman, who turned seventy-six in 2008, is a grandmother of thirteen and great-grandmother of seven. She has won more races than she can count. Her biggest

EVE FLETCHER

EVE FLETCHER GOT HER START SURFING IN 1957 ON A BALSA-WOOD BOARD SHE BORROWED FROM A FAMILY FRIEND, JOHNNY SHEFFIELD, WHO PLAYED "BOY" IN THE OLD TARZAN MOVIES. FLETCHER, THEN A THIRTY-YEAR-OLD ANIMATION ARTIST AT DISNEY STUDIOS, BECAME ONE OF THE FEW WOMEN RIDING THE WAVES EVERY WEEKEND AT SAN ONOFRE BEACH, A SLICE OF UNSPOILED COAST TUCKED BENEATH THE BLUFFS AT SAN DIEGO COUNTY'S NORTHERN EDGE.

"I DON'T THINK YOU CAN BE TOO OLD TO BE STOKED."

On Thursday nights, Fletcher would pack her surfboard and sleeping bag in the car so she could drive from Burbank down to "Sano" right after work on Friday. She'd camp out with her friends and then hit the surf when the sun came up. No one had wet suits back then, so Fletcher suited up on chilly mornings in tights and a shrunken cashmere sweater, then paddled out.

At first the guys in the water gave her a hard time for being out there. Fletcher, though, soon gained acceptance in the Sano tribe for a simple reason: she had nerve.

No matter how fierce the swell, Fletcher, who stands all of five-foot-three, would set her board at an angle and take off with fearless determination. Once she committed to a wave, she always went for it. Her gutsy style earned her respect and a permanent spot in the San Onofre Beach Club.

"I was a water girl," she says, her bright blue eyes sparkling. "I just loved the ocean."

More than a half century later, at age eighty-one, Eve Fletcher is still hanging ten at the same beach with her friends, still impressing everyone with her nerve.

She is retired and living in Laguna Beach these days, still as deeply tanned as in her first days of surfing, with muscle tone that women half her age envy. Her house, sitting on a half-acre lot surrounded by her beloved flower gardens, is a thirty-minute drive from Sano. Three days a week, Fletcher hoists her nine-foot Infinity board and makes her way along the rocky shore.

On a crisp and sunny spring morning, Fletcher paddles into the waves to join about two dozen other surfers lazing in the lineup. The bright red hood of her wet suit makes her easy to spot, and she soon catches three good rides. Fletcher cuts a graceful figure with a steady balance as she glides toward shore. A teenage girl in the water sidles up to ask her, "Can you tell me how to catch a wave?"

Later on the beach, Fletcher showers off and heads back to her Subaru wagon, still lugging that enormous board. "When you get older, you get a bigger board," she says. "It's harder to carry but easier to paddle." She stashes it in the car and then settles behind the hatch in Sano's unpaved lot to share a favorite surf-day ritual with friend Ross McAdam.

"First surfing and then tea," Fletcher says.

"Eve is the prime purveyor of hot water," explains McAdam, a seventy-eight-year-old retired teacher and businessman.

On cue, Fletcher produces a thermos, peppermint tea bags, a jar of honey, and a handful of mugs from the back of her car. Over tea and fresh orange slices, Fletcher and McAdam reminisce about the characters they've known at Sano, the summertime barbecues, and the decades of antics on the sand. Now they are part of the "Geezers"—a group of seven friends, all over sixty-five, who regularly surf at Sano and get together for lunch to celebrate one another's birthdays. "The rules are you have to be eligible for Social Security to join," says McAdam.

Fletcher is the only wahine in the Geezers, but that's nothing new.

She has gained new notoriety among the group since taking a star turn in *Surfing for Life*, a 2001 documentary profiling ten surfing pioneers ages sixty to ninety-four. The film declared San Onofre to be "the home of more surfers over seventy than any other beach in the world," and the regulars say that sounds about right. As Fletcher once told an interviewer, "I don't think you can be too old to be stoked."

"I WAS A
WATER GIRL,"
SHE SAYS,
HER BRIGHT
BLUE EYES SPARKLING.
"I JUST LOVED
THE OCEAN."

GRANVILLE COGGS

DR. GRANVILLE COGGS ARRIVES AT WORK BY 6:20 A.M., FRESH FROM
LAPS IN HIS BACKYARD POOL AND EARLY ENOUGH TO NAB THE SAME
PARKING SPACE AT BROOKE ARMY MEDICAL CENTER THAT HIS CHRYSLER
ALWAYS OCCUPIES—THE SPACE THAT'S PRECISELY 420 METERS TO THE
HOSPITAL'S FRONT DOOR.

With a click of his stopwatch, he's sprinting from the car to the office on a summer morning, always determined to shave off a few precious seconds from the previous morning's run. His best parking lot time so far: 2:20. "If I can run that every day, then when it's time, I can run that in a race," he says.

improve his fitness. Unlike his wife, though, Coggs had never been a high school athlete back in the river delta country of Pine Bluff, Arkansas. Nor had he played sports while working on his undergraduate degree at the University of Nebraska, nor, later, at Harvard med.

Coggs now has a coach, a former U.S. Olympian. He tailors his workouts to fit his schedule as a radiologist at Brooke and other hospitals where he fills in for a few weeks or months at a time.

When he isn't seeing patients, exercising, or playing a homemade washtub bass—the "gut bucket"—Coggs is working on his book, *How to Be Fit at Eighty*. The doctor has a trilogy in mind—sequels would be called *How to be Fit at Ninety* and, later, *How to be Fit at One Hundred*.

He says he intends to follow in the footsteps of his own extraordinary father, Tandy Washington Coggs, the son of former slaves, who grew up to be the president of Arkansas Baptist College and saw all five of his own children graduate from college with advanced degrees.

"He lived to 105," says Coggs, "and I'm a competitor.

"I like to be associated with excellence. Whatever it is, I like to do it to the best of my ability."

"I LIKE TO BE ASSOCIATED WITH EXCELLENCE. WHATEVER IT IS, I LIKE TO DO IT TO THE BEST OF MY ABILITY."

Coggs, who celebrated his eighty-third birthday in July of 2008, is a Texas radiologist who specializes in breast cancer screening. He's a graduate of Harvard University Medical School (the only black student in the class of 1953). He's a former military pilot who flew with the famed Tuskegee Airmen during World War II, earning him a Congressional Gold Medal in 2007. And when he hit his seventies, he really went to work: Coggs became a track star.

He took up running in 1994 after he was diagnosed with narcolepsy and found himself needing naps during the daytime. His wife, Maud, a college sprinter and varsity basketball player, suggested he

So he started slowly, just jogging with his wife in their San Antonio neighborhood before work each morning. Coggs's health improved—and so did his running times. By June 1996, he could run a mile in under eight minutes. The following year, at age seventy-two, he entered the Texas Senior Games and won his first gold medal in the 1500-meter run. That victory sent him to the national games for the first time, and he enjoys going back every two years.

"The people you see at the National Senior Games look young for their ages and they act that way, too," he says. "There's no question about it: it's a lifestyle."

DR. GRANVILLE COGGS'S LONGEVITY PLAN

// Select long-lived parents.

// Engage in aerobic activity.

// Eat a healthy, high-fiber, low-calorie, low-fat diet.

// Take vitamin and mineral supplements.

// Don't smoke, do drugs, or abuse alcohol.

// Be married. (He's been with wife, Maud, for sixty-two years.)

// Have a sense of humor.

// Get enough sleep.

// Wear seat belts and shoulder straps.

SISTER
MADONNA BUDER

PEOPLE CALL HER THE IRON NUN. THE FLYING NUN. THE TRI-ING NUN—
AS IN TRIATHLON. STRANGERS SEE HER PREPARING FOR A RACE, PULLING
ON A WET SUIT OVER THOSE SLENDER SEVENTY-EIGHT-YEAR-OLD LEGS,
AND THEY RUSH UP BEGGING TO POSE BESIDE HER FOR PHOTOS. IT'S AS
IF THEY HOPE SOME OF HER MAGIC WILL RUB OFF.

"You're our hero," gushes a trio of twenty-something men who competed alongside her at a Washington state race. "Can I hug you?" asks a young dad hovering nearby with two small children. Sister Madonna Buder happily obliges, though she remains mostly oblivious to the hubbub that inevitably follows wherever she goes, and that she never anticipated when she first found her vocation as a Catholic nun. At twenty-three, she pledged a quiet life of service over the objections of her well-to-do family in St. Louis.

A quarter century later, a new calling found her. She was on retreat when a priest suggested running as a way to harmonize body, mind, and soul. The idea intrigued her, and Sister Madonna began jogging the very next day in a pair of hand-me-down sneakers. Just five weeks later, in the spring of 1978, at age forty-seven, she signed up for Spokane's 7.4-mile Bloomsday run. Dedicating the race to a family member struggling with alcoholism, she surprised herself by finishing fourth among three hundred women.

Her spirit had been willing. Now Sister Madonna knew she had a gift. God was telling her to run.

Other nuns were scandalized. Running around in shorts? Athletic competitions as religious vocation? Sister Madonna is not the sort of person to back down when she makes up her mind, but she confesses it did help when her bishop gave his blessing for her to run the Boston Marathon in 1982. "All he said was 'Sister, I wish some

of my priests would do what you're doing,'" she recalls. She dedicated the race as a multiple sclerosis fund-raiser. She returned to Boston the next year and again ran for the same cause.

"YOU DON'T NEED TO APOLOGIZE FOR **THE GIFTS YOU'VE BEEN GIVEN.** ONLY APOLOGIZE FOR NOT USING THEM."

Then, Sister Madonna heard about an upcoming triathlon, a grueling endurance contest of running, biking, and swimming. A new challenge! She had enjoyed swimming and riding her bicycle as a child growing up in the Midwest, so she decided to expand her workout. A friend found a clunker of a bike at a police auction, and she was off to train and also to ride back and forth to church.

The daily rigors of pushing herself further than she thought possible—competing with herself as well as other athletes—quickly

became woven into the fabric of Sister Madonna's life. Her athletic ministry became as integral to her world as serving as a eucharistic minister at Mass, studying to earn two master's degrees, and counseling inmates each week at the Spokane County Jail. She says that exercise helps her keep balance in her life and that God, her constant companion, gives her the strength to keep going when her will falters and her legs start to buckle. "I'm sure he does hand-pick certain people for certain things. You can certainly ask, Why me? But I never do."

A trim, soft-spoken woman who wears a simple silver cross atop her bright blue track suit, Sister Madonna has competed in more than three hundred triathlons across the United States, Canada, Australia, and New Zealand. Three dozen of those races have been elite Ironman events, the top tier of triathlon competitions. She's broken records in every age-group category.

Sister Madonna has tackled the Hawaiian Ironman, the godfather of all triathlons, more than twenty times. The Kona race begins with a 2.4-mile rough ocean swim, moves to a 112-mile bike trek through lava fields whipped by vicious headwinds, and concludes with a 26.2-mile marathon to the finish line.

In 2005, Sister Madonna opened the competition's first-ever division for women ages seventy-five to seventy-nine; she is especially proud of breaking that barrier for older women athletes. "Bless the Lord. Praise His Holy Name," she chants as she races, offering encouragement to fellow triathletes struggling along the punishing course.

She says the extraordinary camaraderie among the athletes who come to Hawaii brings her back year after year. In the Ironman, she says, "you experience the highs and the lows, and your vulnerability, and your ability to overcome your own weaknesses."

Over the years, Sister Madonna has broken her right arm six times, her left arm twice, and three of her toes. She has shattered her jaw, scapula, and clavicle and landed in the ER to have her skull sewn up after bike mishaps. In 1984, she fractured her hip so severely that her doctor initially said she might never walk again. Sister Madonna resumed racing several months later.

After each injury, naysayers pointedly ask, *What do you think God is trying to tell you?*

Sister Madonna responds with her sweet smile and answers with a question of her own: "Do you think St. Paul stopped riding his horse when he got knocked off?"

She'd much rather talk about her next goal. "I'm going to keep trying to do the Ironman until I open a new age group." The eighty-and-over Ironman honors await the arrival of Sister Madonna Buder.

"You don't need to apologize for the gifts you've been given. Only apologize for not using them."

BILL CUNNINGHAM & JANE HESSELGESSER

SHE IS A CONCERT PIANIST FROM BALTIMORE, A FORMER BALLERINA, AND A DOCTOR'S WIFE WHO HAD NEVER LIFTED WEIGHTS AND NEVER EVEN SET FOOT IN A GYM UNTIL AGE FIFTY-TWO.

HE IS A BELFAST-BORN SOCCER PLAYER TURNED HOLLYWOOD STUNT-MAN, A DOUBLE FOR TEEN IDOL FRANKIE AVALON IN THOSE CLASSIC 1960S SURF MOVIES WHO BECAME PERSONAL TRAINER TO THE STARS AT THE BEVERLY HILLS HEALTH CLUB.

"I LIVE IN **THE MOMENT.**"

They met in 1998, the beginning of a beautiful partnership.

For the past decade, seventy-two-year-old Bill Cunningham and sixty-two-year-old Jane Hesselgesser have pumped iron together and, for the past six years, competed together in bodybuilding contests around the world. The Southern California duo has won more than two hundred weight-lifting awards, including a gold medal at the Natural Olympia competition in Greece in November 2007. Hesselgesser won a second gold medal in Greece in the division for women ages sixty to sixty-nine.

In competition, the pair's sculpted and deeply bronzed bodies move in unison through a series of choreographed poses that flow with Natalie Cole's song "I Wish You Love." Cunningham brings decades of fitness training to the routine. Hesselgesser injects an exuberant energy and effortless grace from her years as a dancer and musician.

"It's more than just showing a muscle. It's the passion . . . . It's something that is beautiful," says Cunningham.

"We look at it as art," says Hesselgesser.

When they're not competing together, Cunningham and Hesselgesser team up as business partners, working as personal trainers in San Fernando Valley's Westlake Village. They see resistance training as an ideal activity for people over fifty, whom they encourage to start slow and gradually build up endurance and strength. Their clients are for the most part after fitness, not serious bodybuilding, and range from twenty-somethings to a woman who is training to run the Los Angeles Marathon for her eighty-fifth birthday.

"Bodybuilding is the number one sport that you can say prevents disease," says Cunningham, touting the benefits of weight training in boosting the immune system, warding off osteoporosis, and keeping ligaments and tendons flexible.

Hesselgesser had never lifted weights until her husband started working out with Cunningham. One day she decided to tag along to watch her husband's exercise session, and she was impressed with the trainer's fitness program.

Wearing flip-flops and unsure of how to use the gym's machines, Hesselgesser soon found herself working her way through the maze of weight-training devices, with Cunningham as a genial and encouraging mentor. By the end of her first workout, Hesselgesser was hooked. And Cunningham invited her back—making just one request in his lilting Irish accent: "Do you think you could get yourself a pair of gym shoes, love?"

Hesselgesser still laughs when she talks about how she "flip-flopped" her way into a hobby and later a life-changing career as she gradually cut back her music sessions and spent more and more time at the gym.

She and Cunningham follow a strict exercise regime to maintain their fitness and form for competitions. On Mondays and Thursdays, their intensive workouts focus on chests, backs, and arms; on Tuesdays and Fridays, it's all about working the shoulders, triceps, legs, and abdominal areas. When Hesselgesser is getting ready for a competition, she moves outdoors to lunge uphill while carrying dumbbells and takes off for stretches walking backward.

Diet is key to Cunningham's regime. Breakfast is oatmeal with flaxseed oil, flax meal, fresh strawberries, a protein drink, and a rice drink. He sips a protein drink for a mid-morning snack and takes a complement of vitamins and minerals daily. Lunch is salmon, brown rice, and a salad. Dinner typically is more salmon, perhaps with broccoli, a sweet potato, and an apple for dessert. Cunningham says he likes to eat salmon twice a day because it's high in protein and extremely high in essential omega-6 oils, which is "the name of the game for the immune system."

"My lifestyle isn't built around longevity, it's built around health," he says. "I live in the moment. My exercise age, and I don't mean to brag, is late twenties, early thirties. I don't know what it's like to be seventy-two."

Hesselgesser also enjoys a salmon-rich diet; her indulgence is plain yogurt with berries. "I'm healthier now than I was in my thirties or forties," she says.

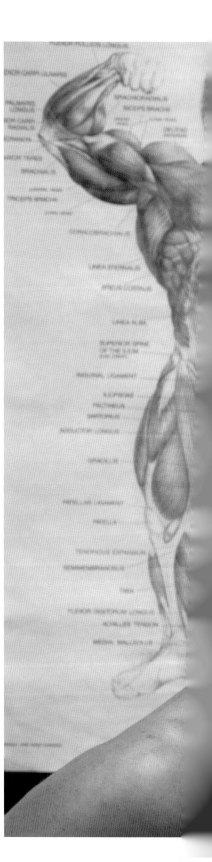

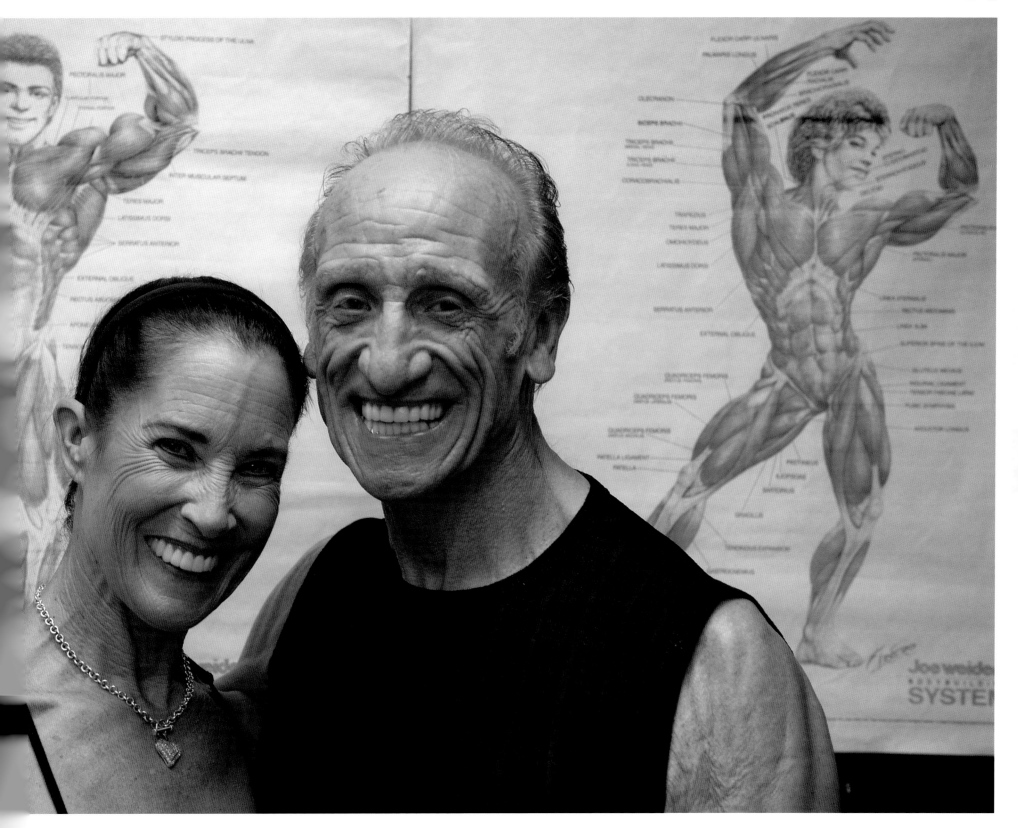

THE AQUADETTES

THEY RANGE IN AGE FROM FIFTY-FOUR TO NINETY-THREE. ON LAND, THEY GRAPPLE WITH BACK TROUBLES AND BAD KNEES AND ACHY-BREAKY HIP REPLACEMENTS. ONE SUFFERS FROM MULTIPLE SCLEROSIS, WHICH MAKES EVEN A FEW STEPS A STRUGGLE.

"THERE'S NO WEIGHT. THERE'S NO PAIN. IT'S JUST SO WONDERFUL, SO HEALING."

But in the water? That's another story. When the Aquadettes squad slips into the swimming pool, the transformation is instantaneous and breathtaking. The women glide and tumble and whirl through the water in graceful formations as show tunes blast from underwater speakers and crowds add their applause.

"There's no weight. There's no pain. It's just so wonderful, so healing," says Valerie Andrews-Link, who at fifty-four is the group's youngest water ballerina and one of the Aquadettes' choreographers. "If people in their nineties can do it, anybody can."

The Aquadettes train all year for the summertime Aqua Follies, a four-performance extravaganza that sells out every August at Southern California's sprawling Laguna Woods senior community. The water ballet dates back to 1965, when a group of residents and lifeguards at what was then Leisure World started swimming together and put on a simple performance.

The show became a summertime tradition as the Aquadettes grew into a well-organized synchronized swimming team, drawing on retirees from across the country who had settled in Laguna Woods. They added coaches, choreographers, lavish costumes, and a supporting cast of "Aquadudes," male friends and family members who help with lighting, sound, ticket sales, and narrating the ninety-minute show. Away from the pool, a team of Aquadette seamstresses works throughout the year to create about a hundred costumes for each season's follies. On performance nights, volunteer "stuffers" stand by to help the showgirls quickly change outfits in between numbers—a crowd-pleasing mix of classical music, Broadway tunes, western songs, marches, and patriotic favorites. Tickets cost just five dollars.

"The process of doing it all is the most fun," says seventy-eight-year-old Beverly Margolis, the show's director and an Aquadette since 1990. "The show is just the icing on the cake."

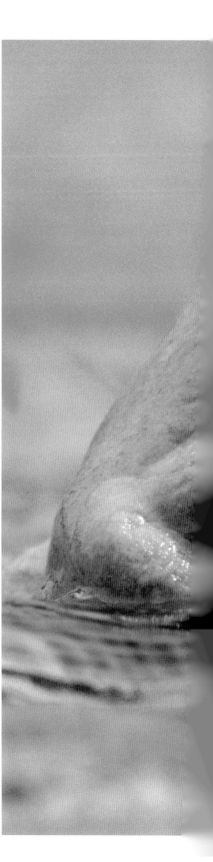

PHIL MULKEY

ON THE MORNING OF HIS SEVENTY-FIFTH BIRTHDAY, PHIL MULKEY THREW DOWN THE GAUNTLET TO A GYM FILLED WITH TEENAGE ATHLETES. THE HIGH SCHOOL TRACK COACH, SENIOR OLYMPICS CHAMPION, AND FORMER U.S. OLYMPIC POLE VAULTER DROPPED TO THE FLOOR AND POWERED THROUGH A HUNDRED PUSH-UPS AS THE KIDS WATCHED IN AMAZEMENT.

Then he repeated the performance—another hundred push-ups, nonstop—for his next class.

"That's my birthday challenge," Mulkey says with a chuckle. "What that tells them is that even at my age I can do it—and so can you."

The challenge is vintage Mulkey. He's been a scrapper all of his life, always ready to face off against anyone, any time, in a dizzying array of athletic events, beginning with the footrace he entered at age fourteen after a friend signed him up without asking. He had never raced before and came away with the silver medal.

Growing up on a Missouri farm, Mulkey was an enterprising kid who turned a pitchfork handle into a javelin, a plow disk into a discus, and bamboo rods into vaulting poles so he could hurl himself onto the garage roof. "I didn't have a pit to land in," he says, "so I used the garage."

As a scrawny five-foot-ten teenager, he hustled his way into a basketball scholarship at the University of Wyoming, playing for two seasons until a six-foot-ten opponent crashed down on his knee during a game in his sophomore year. "That put me out of basketball, so I concentrated on track and field."

For the next twelve years, Mulkey chased an Olympic dream. He poured his boundless energy into pole vault, long jump, shot put, and discus events. In 1960, he made the U.S. decathlon team and went to the Olympic Games in Rome (though a last-minute pulled groin muscle left him unable to make a final vault en route to a medal).

Twenty-seven years later, at age fifty-four, Mulkey turned up at the first-ever National Senior Games in St. Louis in 1987. He was as fierce and fired up as ever, now vaulting on the sport's flexible fiberglass poles and ready to take on all challengers. One of the few former Olympians to compete in the National Senior Games, Mulkey returned to the

He talks to his students about discipline and courage, about absorbing pain and learning from both wins and losses. Since 2002, when he resumed coaching full time, Altamont's track and field teams have won state championships every year.

The coach says his players, in turn, inspire him to keep up his own fitness routine. In the morning he does twenty-

"IF I'M GOING TO LIVE," HE SAYS, "I WANT TO BE **HEALTHY** AND **GOOD LOOKING.**"

Senior Olympics seven more times and battled in countless other track and field contests around the world, often breaking records along the way. Throughout, he also ran a series of small businesses in Marietta, Georgia.

Mulkey, a father of four, grandfather of four, and great-grandfather of two, retired from the business world in 1989, but that didn't last. To his surprise, he was invited back to coach at a Birmingham, Alabama, prep school where he had previously worked in the early 1970s. A flattered Mulkey accepted the job at the Altamont School ("It keeps me in cigarette and whiskey money," he likes to say) and eagerly shares his insights from more than a half century of topflight competitions.

five sit-ups and twenty-five push-ups. Each evening he does twenty-five more of each. He also lifts weights and pedals his stationary bike while watching TV. (He's a big *American Idol* fan.) "If I'm going to live," he says, "I want to be healthy and good looking."

Mulkey's move to Birmingham also inspired him to dig out the medals he had stuffed in shoe boxes over the decades. The walls of his home office and hallway are now covered with three thousand of his awards, including that first silver medal he won at age fourteen.

"I loved to do it all," he says. "I just had this great desire to excel at everything."

PHILIPPA RASCHKER

PHILIPPA RASCHKER IS AN ACCOUNTANT FROM MARIETTA, GEORGIA. SHE ALSO IS A SPRINTER, JUMPER, AND HURDLER WHOSE FEATS INCLUDE TWELVE WORLD RECORDS, THIRTY-ONE AMERICAN RECORDS, TEN WORLD CHAMPIONSHIP GOLD MEDALS, AND TWENTY-SEVEN GOLD MEDALS AT FIVE U.S. NATIONAL CHAMPIONSHIP MEETS.

THAT WAS JUST IN 2007.

"Her accomplishments for the past year would be a lifetime achievement for most other athletes," said the Atlanta Sports Council, which honored Raschker in February 2008 as the city's Amateur Athlete of the Year.

Raschker turned sixty-one the same month she was feted by her hometown. She doesn't keep track of her awards: "I don't ever remember because when it's done, it's done." But she considers the sports council honor an especially memorable one—because it usually goes to a male or female athlete less than half her age.

"She's really unbelievable," says former U.S. Olympian Phil Mulkey, Raschker's former coach and longtime friend. "She's sixty-one and she looks forty-one. She never fails to blow everybody away."

Born in Hamburg, Germany, Raschker was a natural athlete as a child. She delighted in swimming and gymnastics as a toddler and later competed in track and field events at school. At age twenty, Raschker came to the United States to work as a nanny for a family in Washington, D.C. She still enjoyed sports, but found few outlets for serious training. "Back then, there wasn't any place I could do it," she says. "I was out of high school and not associated with a college."

She moved to Massachusetts, where she worked as a meat cutter at a grocery store, though she still longed to race as she had done as a young girl. Her turning point came in 1979, when she happened to read about a master's track event for amateur athletes in Raleigh, North Carolina. The following year, at age thirty-three, she entered the competition.

Since then she has earned a reputation as a relentless competitor who constantly sets new goals—and then bests herself over and over. In 2007, the World Masters Athletics Association named Raschker Female World Masters Athlete of the Year.

She was inducted into the National Senior Games' Hall of Fame in Pittsburgh in 2005. She cites the award as a career highlight. Two years later, she returned to the 2007 National Senior Games in Louisville, where she set one world record (400-meter run), two U.S. records (long jump and triple jump), and seven meet records. "What I like about the Senior Games is that you have athletes of all calibers," she says. "You have athletes that come out for the first time, and it's so nice to see them excel. The Senior Games are one big happy family. When you go there, you see the athletes, and their whole family usually comes along, too. I enjoy that."

Raschker continues to compete for the sheer joy of it and because she likes to stay fit. She has a hard time choosing events at competitions, so she often does them all. She ticks off the list of events that she qualified for during 2008 for the 2009 Senior Games in the San Francisco Bay Area: 100-meter, 200-meter, 400-meter, and 800-meter races, plus the high jump, long jump, triple jump, pole vault, discus throw, and javelin throw. "My springs and jumps—I love them all," she says.

In the next breath, she mentions—quite seriously—that she thinks she may be slowing down. But that's okay, she says, because an athlete has to know her limits, to know that sometimes she needs

"AS I GET OLDER, **LESS IS MORE.**"

to train her hardest and that on certain days it's okay to forgo a workout. After a breakfast of oatmeal and fruit, she runs three mornings a week during warmer months; in winter she cuts back to runs two days a week and puts a stronger emphasis on weight training. She says many athletes overtrain and that she has learned over the years to work smarter.

"As I get older, less is more," she says. "I always try to listen to my body. I've done it for so many years that I can be honest with myself."

NATIONAL GEOGRAPHIC MAGAZINE DISPATCHED RICK TO MONTANA IN 1989 TO PHOTOGRAPH THE GREAT CENTENNIAL CATTLE DRIVE, A FIVE-DAY HORSE-BACK TREK ACROSS THE PRAIRIE FROM ROUNDUP TO BILLINGS. THAT'S WHERE RICK FIRST MET CHARLIE SIMS, A SIXTY-SOMETHING COWBOY WHO HAD A REPUTATION AMONG HIS PEERS AS A ROPER AND WRANGLER EXTRAORDINAIRE. EVERY MORNING AT SUNRISE, SIMS CORRALLED THE HORSES INTO CAMP, DEFTLY LASSOED EACH ONE, AND THEN SADDLED UP THE HORSES FOR THE RIDERS. "IT WAS A CLASSIC CATTLE DRIVE, JUST LIKE IN THE OLD DAYS. THEY WERE PUSHING CATTLE ACROSS THE STATE, AND THE ONLY WAY I COULD GET PICTURES WAS TO RIDE AND SHOOT," RICK SAYS. "THE OTHER COWBOYS WERE SWINGING LARIATS, BUT NONE OF THEM COULD SWING A LARIAT LIKE CHARLIE SIMS. HE WAS ALWAYS WORKING THAT ROPE. YOU KNOW HOW A BASKETBALL PLAYER HAS TOTAL CONTROL OVER A BALL? WELL, CHARLIE HAD TOTAL CONTROL OF THE ROPE. HE COULD JUST MAKE IT SING."

CHARLIE SIMS

WILD OLD WOMEN

IN THE SUMMER OF 2002, RESEARCHER JENIFER MASON ORGANIZED AN UNUSUAL SWIM PARTY: SHE INVITED SIX SAN DIEGO WOMEN IN THEIR SIXTIES ON A TWENTY-ONE-MILE TREK FROM CATALINA ISLAND TO THE SOUTHERN CALIFORNIA MAINLAND.

THE WILD OLD WOMEN HAD SET A WORLD RECORD, BECOMING **THE OLDEST GROUP TO SWIM THE CATALINA CHANNEL** AS A RELAY EVENT.

At 4:34 AM on July 8, team captain Carol Sing dove into the surf off Catalina's Doctor's Beach with only glow sticks lighting her way in the darkness. An emergency medical technician hovered nearby in a kayak as sixty-year-old Sing swam the first leg for her team, the Wild Old Women (WOW).

A fishing boat served as the team's floating base camp and the other women—Deborah Peckham, sixty-two; Betsy Jordan, sixty-five; Sandra Vickers, sixty-three;

Adrienne Pipes, sixty-eight; and Janet Lamott, sixty-six—took turns in the rough and chilly sixty-five-degree waters of the Pacific Ocean. Mason, the president of the Center for Activity Research and Education in Dallas, had invited Rick along to document their relay marathon. He manned a second kayak, photographing the women as they swam in pairs through the waves.

Finally, jubilantly, Vickers came ashore in Palos Verdes at 3:09 PM—ten hours and thirty-five minutes after the marathon

began. The Wild Old Women had set a world record, becoming the oldest group to swim the Catalina Channel as a relay event. "These six women feel passionately that participating in an event such as this brings attention to a 'new image of aging' and because it's fun," says Mason.

Her next project: raising money for another group relay swim, this time across the English Channel.

BEA THOMAS

IN HER TEENS, BEA THOMAS EMBARKED ON A GROUNDBREAKING ATHLETIC CAREER THAT HAS SPANNED MORE THAN SEVENTY YEARS. SHE WAS AN ALL-AMERICAN FIELD HOCKEY PLAYER AT TEMPLE UNIVERSITY IN PHILADELPHIA IN THE 1930S AND WENT ON TO BECOME A GOALIE FOR THE U.S. NATIONAL SQUAD. SHE PLAYED FIELD HOCKEY WELL INTO HER SIXTIES AND TAUGHT GENERATION AFTER GENERATION OF YOUNG GIRLS HOW TO PLAY COMPETITIVE SPORTS. THOMAS HELPED BUILD A POWERHOUSE FIELD HOCKEY PROGRAM AT MOORESTOWN HIGH SCHOOL IN NEW JERSEY, WHERE THE KIDS CALLED HER "MRS. T."

"SHE LIVED BY THE THREE Ds— **DESIRE, DETERMINATION,** AND **DEDICATION.**"

In 1998, the United States Field Hockey Association named Thomas Developmental Coach of the Year, noting her work with Moorestown's undefeated field hockey and lacrosse teams. "Thomas is an American classic at age eighty-seven," the association said in announcing her award. She also served as the school's varsity swim coach. Thomas continued as the goalie coach at Moorestown until 2004, when she retired at age ninety-two and moved to New Hampshire. "She was an inspiration and a big motivator," says Joan Lewis, a close friend and fellow coach for many years. "She lived by the three Ds—desire, determination, and dedication."

Thomas celebrated her ninety-sixth birthday in the summer of 2008.

The Washington D.C. delegation arrives in Baton Rouge in 1993.

SCENES FROM THE NATIONAL SENIOR GAMES

EVERY TWO YEARS, THOUSANDS OF ATHLETES FROM ACROSS THE UNITED STATES CONVERGE ON THE LARGEST SPORTING EVENT IN THE WORLD FOR MEN AND WOMEN OVER FIFTY: THE NATIONAL SENIOR GAMES.

Participants compete in these Senior Olympics for medals in eighteen sports: archery, badminton, basketball, bicycling, bowling, golf, horseshoes, race walking, racquetball, road race, shuffleboard, softball, swimming, table tennis, tennis, track and field, triathlon, and volleyball.

The games have exploded in size and intensity since 1987, when 2,500 senior athletes gathered in St. Louis. In August 2009, more than 12,000 seniors were expected to compete as the national games came to the West Coast for the first time, hosted by the Stanford University campus in the San Francisco Bay Area.

The biennial summer games inevitably set new national and world records, and new achievements worthy of recognition in the National Senior Games' Hall of Fame. "This idea of a bunch of old people running around in colored underwear doesn't fit what's going on," says 1960 U.S. Olympian Phil Mulkey, who has competed—and set new records— in track and field events at the National Senior Games since 1987.

To reach the Senior Games, athletes must first qualify in state competitions held the previous year. Qualifying requirements vary from sport to sport, but an athlete must be a top finisher (usually first, second, or third place) in an age group to make the nationals. About 350,000 men and women vie at the local and state levels to earn a golden ticket to the National Senior Games, according to Jenifer Mason, a trustee of the NSGA Foundation. She notes that two-thirds of Senior Games participants indicated that they had not been physically active before age fifty.

Along with qualifying events, the summertime games also feature demonstration events: equestrian, fencing, lawn bowling, rowing, sailing, soccer, and water polo.

In 2008, the nonprofit National Senior Games Association added a fall championship festival in Rhode Island, where athletes faced off in billiards, team bowling, hockey, pickleball, and weight-lifting events. Providence mayor David N. Cicilline

heralded the fall competition by proclaiming, "Sixty really is the new forty."

Mark Zeug, chairman of the National Senior Games Association and president of the Hawaii Senior Games Association, says that he sees the NSGA expanding in the future to offer noncompetitive fitness programs and mental fitness challenges, as well as more international senior competitions. Regular physical activity has tangible benefits that cannot be overstated.

"You can expect to live up to ten years longer if you stay physically active; you can expect to save about $3,600 per year on medical and pharmaceutical costs by staying active in your senior years; you will be better able to combat illness when it does strike; you will be healthier and happier and enjoy life more if you stay physically active," Zeug told the White House Council on Aging in 2005.

"We all know it, and our seniors prove it every time they lace up their running shoes, or pick up a tennis racquet."

THE NATIONAL SENIOR GAMES: BY THE NUMBERS

YEAR	LOCATION	ATHLETES PARTICIPATING
1987	St. Louis, MO	2,500
1989	St. Louis, MO	3,400
1991	Syracuse, NY	5,000
1993	Baton Rouge, LA	7,200
1995	San Antonio, TX	8,200
1997	Tucson, AZ	10,300
1999	Orlando, FL	12,000
2001	Baton Rouge, LA	8,700
2003	Hampton Roads, VA	10,700
2005	Pittsburgh, PA	10,500
2007	Louisville, KY	12,100
2009	San Francisco, CA	12,750*
2011	Houston, TX	15,000*

*anticipated. For more information, visit the National Senior Games online: www.nsga.com

OPENING CEREMONIES

>> 1999: *Opening ceremonies in Orlando; the competition was held on the grounds at Disney World in Florida; New Mexico competitors in the Parade of Athletes.*

THE COMPETITORS

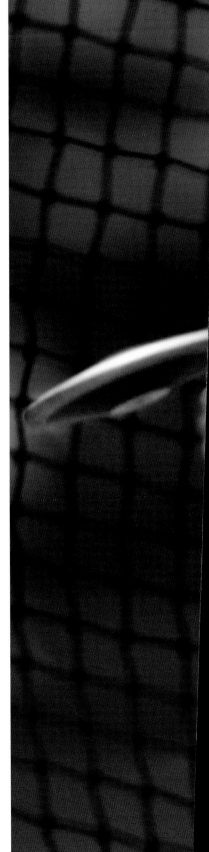

>> *Discus thrower in Baton Rouge (1993)*

MARGARET HINTON // *Hinton lives in Baytown, Texas, and has competed numerous times in the national games. Rick first met her at the National Senior Games in Baton Rouge in 1993 and was impressed with her intense focus. "Margaret told me, 'I can tell that some of these people came here to socialize. That's okay, but I've come here to take home the gold.' True to her word, she was indeed on the medal stand two days later."*

>> ARCHER: *an 80-something competitor in Hampton Roads, Virginia, in 2003*

>> *Details of her arrows in the target*

<< ANOTHER ARCHER: *a slice of how competitors decorate their quivers*

>> TARGETING THE ARROW: *An archer lines up her shot in Hampton Roads, Virginia (2003).*

<< *Pole vaulter Lenora Daniels in an early morning warmup in San Antonio (1995)*

>> *Daniels' friend, Jack Haefel, throws the discus in the same games.*

<< *A first-time competitor from Santa Fe throws the javelin in Baton Rouge (2001).*

>> *An athlete from Montana delights in the long jump in Baton Rouge (1993).*

<< COUPLE: *A wife helps her husband stretch on the practice track as he gets ready for the 1500-meter run in Baton Rouge (2001).*

<< MORE STRETCHING: *An athlete gets ready to run the 100-meter race in Pittsburgh (2005).*

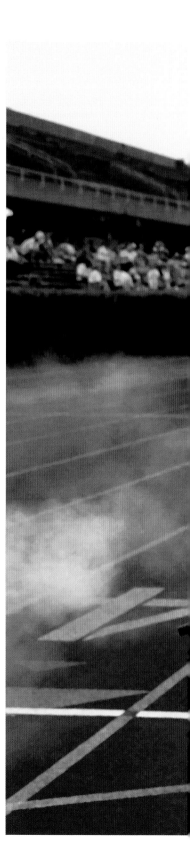

<< CHEERING SQUAD: *Run Grammy Run!*
In Hampton Roads, Virginia (2003)

>> ALLIE WALKER: *She maintains her pace as the*
starter fires his pistol to signal the final lap.

<< *Allie Walker crosses the finish line. She has Parkinson's disease, but that hasn't stopped her from competing over and over in the National Senior Games.*

<< WAITING FOR THE START: *Competitors wish each other luck before the 800-meter run in Hampton Roads, Virginia (2003).*

>> *Helen Beauchamp, a track and field athlete from Ripley, Mississippi, celebrates with her grandson after a race at the Baton Rouge games (2001).*

<< PEDAL POWER: *cycling the race course in Hampton Roads, Virginia (2003)*

>> SWEET VICTORY: *winning her bike race in Hampton Roads, Virginia (2003)*

SWIM SESSIONS

>> ANOTHER TRIATHLON START: *The men rush into*
the water to begin the race in Orlando (1999).

<< TRIATHLON POOL START: *The men take the water in San Antonio (1995).*

>> THE BACKSTROKE: *a competitor at the start of her race in the same games*

ICE HOCKEY

>> ON THE BENCH, IN THE TEAM BOX: *A player roots on his teammates in Minneapolis during the winter hockey competition in 2005.*

WOMEN'S BASKETBALL

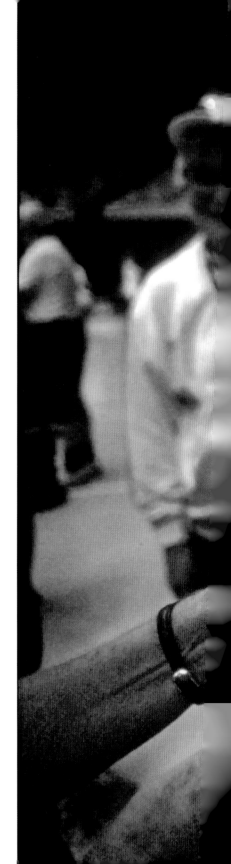

>> PROUD MOMENT: *A member of the Sooner Gals shows off her silver medal in Baton Rouge (2001).*

<< COURT ACTION: *A player on the Sooner Gals from Oklahoma gets ready to shoot. Hampton Roads, Virginia (2003).*

>> *Scrambling for the ball during a game in Pittsburgh (2005)*

MEN'S
BASKETBALL

WOMEN'S SOFTBALL

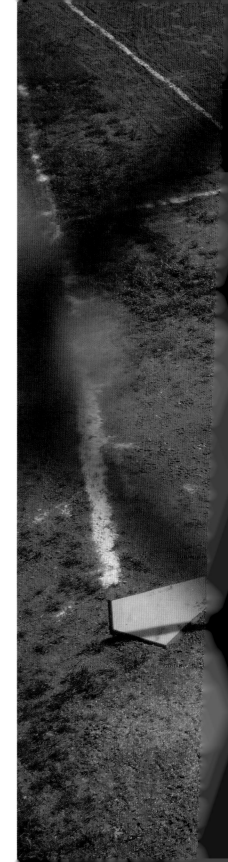

>> *Overview of the softball action as the Golden Girls face a Tucson team in Pittsburgh (2005)*

<< *The Golden Girls warm up before a game during the Pittsburgh games (2005).*

>> GOOD CATCH: *A centerfielder for the Golden Girls reaches for the ball in Pittsburgh (2005).*

<< IN THE STANDS: *A son videotapes his mom on the field and shows support with a custom T-shirt in Hampton Roads, Virginia (2003).*

MEN'S SOFTBALL

>> DRAGON TATTOO: *A player sports a tat and red baseball shoes in Pittsburgh (2005).*

∨ FLYING CATCH: *A player gets down and dirty in Hampton Roads, Virginia (2003).*

TENNIS

A player in a red visor keeps her eye
on the ball in Pittsburgh (2005).

<< LOVE IN THE STANDS: *A Colorado couple shares a sweet moment in San Antonio in 1995. (She's a competitor; he's a spectator.)*

I would like to thank Audrey Jonckheer, for securing funding from Kodak to finance the early years of this project; my dear friend Dave Black, for never letting me forget that finishing this book was one of the most important things I could do in my career; and my grandfather, Jake Kleinhesselink, for always showing me that each day of life should be an adventure. I'd like to include a special tribute to Doug Craig, a legendary surfer at San Onofre Beach who told me in 1998 that I had to stand up on a surfboard before I could take his picture. So I bought a board, learned to surf, and Doug and I became friends. When he passed away in 2004, I joined more than two hundred surfers at his paddle-out memorial service at San Onofre. Doug was eighty-two. I still miss him and I'm still surfing at San Onofre.

// RICK RICKMAN

ACKNOWLEDGMENTS

We are indebted to Kim Grant and Kate Cohen, and we owe a special thank you to our editor, Carey Jones, who believed in *The Wonder Years* from the start. We are so grateful for the help of Ursula Cary, Brooke Johnson, Lawrence Wilson, and Empire Design Studio.

Finally, we'd like to thank all of the extraordinary athletes and adventurers who so generously shared their time and amazing stories with us.

// RICK RICKMAN AND DONNA WARES